Miao

8

INDIGENOUS PEOPLES OF THE WORLD
Miao

Grolier Educational Corporation

SHERMAN TURNPIKE, DANBURY, CONNECTICUT 06816

Published by Grolier Educational Corporation 1995
Danbury, Connecticut

Set ISBN: 0-7172-7470-5
Volume ISBN: *Miao* 0-7172-7476-4
Library of Congress Number 94-079529

Manufactured in the United States of America.

Contributors

Jennifer Croft *(Ladakhi)* holds a degree in anthropology from Columbia University and is an editor and free-lance writer.

Anne Johnson *(Inuit, Karenni, Mentawai, Naga)* holds a degree from the University of Wisconsin, Madison. She has done extensive research on myths and folk epics from around the world.

Barbara Miller *(Tuareg)* is a Ph.D. candidate in anthropology at New York University. She specializes in ethnographic filmmaking. She has conducted applied urban research and has been involved with developing curricula for museums and schools.

Eugene Murphy, Ph.D. *(Maya)* is an instructor of anthropology at Columbia University. He has produced an ethnographic documentary on Mayan migration and has written extensively on the peoples of Mexico and China.

Roger Rosen *(Endangered Peoples)* is an editor and publisher. He has published material on the indigenous peoples of the former Soviet Union and has edited numerous articles and papers on the plight of indigenous peoples.

Steven Rubenstein, Ph.D. *(Huaorani)* has been awarded grants in the field of anthropology from the Guggenheim, Fulbright, and MacArthur Foundations and has conducted fieldwork in Brazil, Ecuador, and the United States.

Colleen She *(Miao)* received a master's degree in East Asian studies from Columbia University. She is a free-lance writer and translator.

Jeanne Strazzabosco *(Wayana)* is an instructor in French and Spanish and a free-lance translator and writer whose work regularly addresses the plight of indigenous peoples.

Pegi Vail *(Omo Peoples)* is a Ph.D. candidate in anthropology at New York University. She specializes in visual anthropology and has worked extensively with children's educational programs at museums and schools.

Contents

Miao children must choose a traditional village life or a more modern existence.

CHAPTER 1

THE BAMBOO FLUTE

FOR YEARS, LITTLE HAD CHANGED IN XIJIANG VILLAGE. THE people made their living by making the earth fruitful. Every year rice was planted, tended, and harvested in harmony with the seasons. There were days of celebration and mundane days of work, which together formed a continuum of existence for the Miao.

One day, something from a distant place came to Xijiang, forever disrupting the simple pattern of life that had existed for several generations. The thing was large and cubical. It became the new symbol of prosperity for the villagers. Everyone congregated at the Tang residence in sheer awe of the television set. Grandmother Tang said it was just like when the villagers first saw a lightbulb.

Young Cheng was mesmerized by the new arrival. For days he sat in front of the screen watching the pretty ladies sell a variety of things of which neither Cheng nor his family had ever heard. Cheng wondered why everyone seemed so unnaturally happy. He asked his father where was this place where everyone was so exuberant. His father, Jian, explained that the people on television were paid to act that way. There was no real place on earth where life could be so perfect.

Despite his father's words, the television had planted a seed in young Cheng's mind. He was too young to be aware that it would compel him to leave Xijiang. Eventually, Cheng would no longer settle for the simple life in the small wooden houses. He would want to work in Shenzhen, one of China's economically thriving cities. He would want to wear sunglasses and feel the power of a different definition of manhood.

Of course, these ideas were not fully formed in the child Cheng. For now, he was perfectly content to live with his family for the rest of his life. He loved Grandma Tang, who doted on him. He loved to watch his mother embroider beautiful flowers on fabric. He felt secure as he watched his father count the many bushels of rice the family produced.

As young Cheng lay bundled in bed, he asked his father to tell him the tale of the Bamboo Pipe (Lusheng). "Why is the bamboo pipe so sacred to us?" he asked. Cheng and his friends had tried to heed parental admonitions about playing near the Lusheng sacred ground. A good number of balls, sticks, and skipping stones had nevertheless made their way onto the Lusheng Ground, to be retrieved only once a year when it was open to the villagers on Bridge Holiday.

Cheng's father, small and agile looking, began to sing. His voice resounded in the delicately built wooden house. The song seemed to pierce the walls. Singing was second nature to

Many Miao families make their living growing rice.

Jian, as it was to all the Miao. Not a day passed without his seeing visitors off with a verse. "Your presence, honored guest, is like a crimson cloud on the horizon. We don't have good dishes, but only good wine. We Miao treat our guests with this generosity." Like many other Miao, Cheng's father made up the words as he went along. He told the story of the Lu-sheng, or Bamboo Pipe. The incantation was rhythmical and transported Cheng into the land of dreams.

Many years ago, Xijiang village was prosperous. Miao women wore clothes made colorful by their own hands. On the clothes were embroidered stories of the heroic Miao past. Under the leadership of Ying Fofeng, we were no longer hunters and gatherers. We filled the marshlands with dirt and planted rice paddies.

The Miao prospered in abundance. Each day from dawn till dusk we toiled under the heavens. Living by the cycles of nature, we celebrated our New Year according to the lunar calendar.

For many years, nature was merciful, and we were happy. Through our songs, we courted the women and won their hearts. Xijiang village flourished.

Then the ominous clouds came and shielded the warmth of the sun. Xijiang was shrouded by clouds so thick that it seemed night had fallen. Our rice paddies bore no crops, and our livestock went hungry. There was no subsistence for the Miao. Many people fell ill.

A village elder of the Xu family, distraught by our tribulations, came up with an ingenious solution. He called the men together to discuss how to disperse the clouds.

"All of our crops have withered. Our livestock are dying. Families suffer excessive dearth. The only thing that stands strong is the wild bamboo, a hearty plant that the Han Chinese have looked to as the symbol of true strength; for the bamboo reaches for the sky and yet is rooted in the ground. It is hollow in the center, as we should be hollow and not filled with pride and arrogance.

"We will use the bamboo to make pipes and blow away the deadly clouds."

The villagers made pipes and tried to blow, but to no avail. Still the sun was not to be seen. One of the villagers believed that Xu was not a good leader, so a new bamboo pipe leader was chosen. In spite of the soothing music pouring from the pipes, the right leader still had not been chosen.

Finally, Tang was chosen. He led an orchestra of pipes that played for three days until the clouds finally dispersed. To this day, the Tangs have led the Miao. No one can blow his pipes on the Lusheng sacred ground without the Tang leader...▲

CHAPTER 2

A MOUNTAIN PEOPLE

SCATTERED ALL OVER ASIA, THE MIAO, OR THE HMONG, AS they are sometimes called, usually dwell in mountainous places. Their villages consist of several households clustered together. Miao of different regions have adopted the ways of life of surrounding peoples. In China alone, there are 7.4 million Miao, making them the fourth-largest minority in China. Some Miao also live in Southeast Asian countries such as Laos and Cambodia, where they are known as Hmong. Miao clans unite when there is a great external threat. In the face of the Han Chinese, the largest ethnic group in China, the Miao have been known to band together. Despite these occasional demonstrations of unity, however, the Miao, as a whole, are joined in a very weak alliance.

The Miao live in simple wooden dwellings nestled in some of the steepest regions of Guizhou and Yunnan provinces. Timber is abundant in this part of China. In the mountainous regions, the Miao build their houses on stilts; in less hilly areas, they live in huts woven of twigs and branches.

The Miao are farmers. Their major crops are rice, maize, potatoes, sorghum, beans, rape, peanuts, tobacco, ramie, sugarcane, and cotton.

Miao Origins

The existence of the Miao has been documented as early as the T'ang and Sung dynasties (618-1279). Their ancestors probably came from present-day Hunan Province. From there, some migrated east to Sichuan Province, and others moved to Guizhou. The name "Miao" is broadly applied, referring to social groups that are often difficult to classify. Miao customs, ways of dressing, and rituals vary according to region.

Legendary heroes of the Miao demonstrate a wide span of beliefs. The Hmong of Laos have completely adopted the belief systems of their host country. They look back to Sin Sai, a legendary figure whom they believe can help people when they need protection. The Miao of China view themselves within the context of their own history. They refer back to the mythical chieftain Ying Fofeng. According to legend, Ying, tired of living as a nomad, led his people to a more settled, agrarian way of life, and the Miao became rice farmers.

Who Are the Miao?

Defining just who the Miao people are is not easy for several reasons. First, it was the Chinese who applied the name "Miao" to the Hmong as well as to the Miao of Guizhou.

The Legend of Sin Sai

In the olden days, about 5,000 years ago, there was only one land. The land was as small as a deer's footprint. There was only one tree. The tree was the size of a small candle. There was only one hermit who dwelled on the land as small as a deer's footprint. When the hermit was 1,000 years old, he molded clay to make a man and a woman. By the work of his magic hand he created Phaou Sank See, the first man, and Ya Sank Sar, the first woman. They lived together for many years and conceived a son, Sin Sai, who was powerful, grateful, and kind.

When Sin Sai became 25, his town was harassed by an ogre who wanted to kill him and his townsfolk. Sin Sai sent a message to the ogre that he wanted to make war. The ogre had eyes like the fires of hell. When he received Sin Sai's message, the ogre growled furiously. He swirled in the sky and created an army of small warrior giants.

Sin Sai said, "Oh, beloved hermit and parents, you are dear to me." He put rice in his mouth and spat it out. Each grain of rice became a soldier, and Sin Sai's army defeated the ogre's army. When the ogre was killed, Sin Sai said, "There is no use for me in the world of men. I will have to go to the other world to kill the evil spirits."

Many Miao make their home in the mountains of China.

A Miao village consists of several households.

The Hmong of Southeast Asia formerly lived in China. They bitterly recall their mid-19th century forced exodus from China.

Even in the 1970s, Hmong leaders in Laos believed that the name Miao meant "slave" in Chinese. Although that is not the case, their rejection of the name demonstrates continued antagonism toward the Chinese. The name Hmong in the Hmong language means "free people." As a minority among the Han Chinese, the Miao have a fierce sense of independence.

Another reason it is difficult to categorize the Miao into one group is geographic spread. Miao settlements are found in isolated pockets throughout southwestern China. Some Miao live in Hainan Province, an island in the South China Sea. In addition, Miao have migrated as far as Laos and Cambodia. Further, not all Miao share a common language. Although there is a Miao dialect, and a Hmong dialect, some Miao in China speak the language of other ethnic minorities.

The Miao are facing modernizing influences. Miao ways of life are fast disappearing. Modern life has transformed the culture and destroyed many traditions.▲

In China, Miao traditions and culture are endangered by modernization.

CHAPTER 3

CUSTOMS AND BELIEFS

HOW IS IT THAT THE MIAO ARE SUCH A VARIED AND scattered people? Perhaps the answer lies in socioeconomic issues. Throughout history, the ethnic minorities of China, including the Miao, have been economically disfranchised social groups. This is the reason the Hmong were forced to leave China. However we classify and attempt to define the Miao, they live a life that is richly colored by folklore, music, and traditions.

Religious Beliefs

The Miao of Guizhou build ancestral shrines, a practice most commonly associated with Chinese beliefs. This suggests that the Miao were influenced by the patriarchal system. However, Miao beliefs are not simply a variation of Chinese beliefs. Some scholars consider their practices polytheist; others believe the Miao are animists. The Hmong of Laos combine animism with shamanism.

Today, Miao youth are influenced heavily by modern Chinese culture as well as by their ancestral traditions.

Family Relations

The Miao of southwestern China live in nuclear, monogamous families. Each member of a family is addressed specifically depending upon his rank within the family and whether the person is from the maternal or paternal side of the extended family. As in many traditional societies, men hold the positions of greatest power and influence. Communities are headed by a respected elder who makes the important decisions and serves as mediator in disputes.

Lusheng and Song

China's urban areas are highly cosmopolitan. Chinese youth prefer Taiwanese pop stars to the grating sounds of Chinese opera. Shanghainese youth would rather frequent the disco than hear the pensive sounds of the zither. The Miao face the same division. As Miao youth migrate out of their villages in search of a higher standard of living, they often leave behind a rich musical tradition.

The Lusheng or bamboo flute is one of the Miao's traditional instruments. The Lusheng Ground is a piece of land in every village that is set aside for the playing of this instrument in the Lusheng ceremonies. The Lusheng was originally used as a kind of bugle to summon young braves to war. It was developed approximately 2,000 years ago. Most Lushengs are made of bamboo and are hand-held. The largest ones are not made of bamboo and must be either rested on the ground or supported by an assistant. A large Lusheng can be heard from several miles away as it sends its magical sound from village to village. The Hmong term for the Lusheng is the Khene. With the departure of young Miao to the cities, some fear that this aspect of Miao culture may gradually be lost.

The Lusheng is only a part of the rich Miao musical tradition. The Miao use song on an almost daily basis to address some of their most basic needs, one of the most significant being love.

Courtship

Miao courting practices vary from group to group. Some Miao still utilize matchmaking, in which parental involvement is key. In the past, the Miao of Yunnan Province "kidnapped" the bride. If she consented to marriage, a wedding banquet was held. "Kidnapping" among the Miao was less a violent act than a ritual that played out a basic desire to select a female mate. Some Miao groups now allow for both parties to have a say in selecting their prospective mates.

Among the Miao, success in courtship may depend upon the ability to serenade a potential boyfriend or girlfriend in public. Not only do the Miao play the Lusheng, but they are expected to be good singers. Teenagers who are interested in each other do not go on dates. They engage in a courtship ritual called *Youfang* or, roughly translated, "making the circuit." It is collective courtship, involving a group of young men and women, with set rules of etiquette. The ritual takes place on holidays, or during the season when there is less work to be

The Lusheng, a bamboo instrument, has been part of the Miao musical tradition for over a thousand years.

done. On these days, young Miao gather and go to the *malang*, or open grounds. There, young men and women publicly declare their love for each other through song. If the attraction is mutual, a firm commitment to complete the courtship ritual is necessary.

Most 15- to 17-year-olds participate in the courtship ritual. All participants and observers are required to applaud the singers. Most of the Miao love songs have been passed down from generation to generation. Some songs, however, are spontaneously created for the occasion. The songs are light and melodious, expressing the delicate feelings of the courting

When Miao girls reach the age of 15, they are able to participate in *Youfang*, a courtship ritual.

young men and women. They are sung at a low pitch, almost a whisper.

"Making the circuit" takes place in the evening. Usually, 100 to 200 young people take part. Spectators come from the locality as well as other villages to witness the event. The grounds are festive, full of singing, laughing, and flirting. The couples are fired with passion. You can find them hand-in-hand expressing mutual admiration through song. The love duets translate something like this:

Boy: Do you find me attractive? If so, let's talk.
Girl: Had I not liked you from the start, I would not have

A Miao man wearing a traditional headdress.

come tonight. When I heard you were coming, I rushed here, while supper was left to cool. I thank you for coming and making me forget my grief.

Boy: Water quenches the fields even as fields soak up water. Your coming eased my anguish.

Girl: Indeed, my anguish is removed by your presence.

Boy: When the fruit is ripe, it is ready to eat. We are ripe, mature enough to fall in love.

Girl: The feeling is mutual.

Boy: Let us make a bridge over the ravine that separates us. Girl meets boy, boy meets girl.

The young couples sing to each other without embarrassment. Although formal rules must be followed, such as not leaving the courting grounds, the atmosphere of *Youfang* is light and romantic. The participants achieve a kind of "love trance," acting as if no one else were present. *Youfang* has been passed down from generation to generation. When a girl reaches the age of ten, she learns the love songs from her mother. The boys learn the songs by observing the actual ritual over and over.

Youfang is a crucial part of finding one's mate. Miao youth participate in the courtship ritual over a course of time until they become acquainted. The final result of *Youfang* is marriage. ▲

Even very young Miao children wear the traditional silver jewelry on holidays.

CHAPTER 4

MIAO TRADITIONS

LARGE INTERNATIONAL CHAIN STORES ARE SETTING THE pace of fashion all over East Asia. Miao youth may soon prefer Western clothing to their bulky and somewhat ceremonial attire. But the Miao have retained a rich tradition in their embroidered works. They are already capitalizing on their talents. Miao handicrafts are produced and marketed widely in cottage industries sponsored by the Chinese government. Some of the Miao women combine their singing and stitching talents by becoming entertainers wearing their own creations.

Most Miao girls learn to embroider when they are five years old. By their teens, they are expected to have mastered a core of basic designs. During courtship, women give their prospective mate a sample of their handiwork as a token. The most exquisite pieces, which can take years to make, are saved for the dowry. Bridal costumes take three to four years to complete.

A number of common themes are found in Miao embroidery: dragons, tigers, lions, and various flora. The patterns are sewn without the aid of embroidery hoops. They are created

All Miao girls begin to learn embroidery when they are five years old.

spontaneously and are embroidered directly onto the fabric without premarking. The designs vary by region and are highly influenced by the host culture. The Miao of Guizhou utilize many themes indigenous to China. Often, the embroidery is so elaborate that it tells an entire story.

An old Guizhou legend explains why Miao women have become so adept at their art: A long time ago, young men used to marry into women's families, leaving home at an appointed time. But the men objected to this practice and would return home soon after marrying, only to dispute with their sisters in the hope of exchanging roles and so being able to stay in their own homes. The siblings became embroiled in an argument. A plowing competition was set to determine who would have to leave home. The men were quickest at plowing, leaving the women no choice but to leave home when married. In concession, the women were allowed to adorn themselves in splendid garb.

The marriage legend remains a popular theme in Miao embroidery today. Anthropologists believe that it reflects a real change in Miao social culture from a matriarchy to a patriarchy.

The *gan mo*, a small insect that inhabits rice paddies, became a favorite theme on Miao bridal attire. It was believed that the *gan mo* gave birth to the dragonfly, symbolizing the flight from home a young woman makes when she marries.

Behind every design on the native Miao costume lies social meaning. The image of a peacock celebrates a woman's desire to please the opposite sex.

The Miao eat large quantities of pickled foods. Above, a woman prepares a meal.

Traditional Miao clothing is brightly colored and elaborately decorated. Every item holds a social meaning.

An old Miao song goes:

"We are smarter men today than we were yesterday.
Though smart we were, who was the smartest of all?
There was a young lad who went high up in the mountains
*   to fetch a peacock for his beloved.*
Instead of the peacock, the lad fetched his own beloved.
The beloved young maiden dressed up as a peacock,
*   thus becoming her own matchmaker.*
With a headdress like the crown of the peacock, the ample
*   embroidery of her gown became as peacock wings.*
The maiden's wide sleeves were the majestic feathers.
How much like peacocks are the Miao maidens!"

Rice and fish are staple foods in the Miao diet. The fish are raised in the rice paddies.

The Pickle Jar

Pickled foods are a central part of the Miao diet. In their steep, inaccessible mountain villages, salt has always been a valuable commodity. Pickling allows the Miao to conserve salt by using only enough to keep food from spoiling. Every Miao household has a large earthen pickle jar, and many foods are pickled.

The Miao raise fish in their rice paddies. Every spring, just after the rice seedlings are transplanted, minnows are let loose in the paddies. A symbiotic relationship develops between the young fish and the rice plants. By the autumn harvest, not only is the rice ready to be harvested, but the fish are fully grown. Outside of the few fish that are eaten fresh, the majority must be pickled.

The Miao also raise pigs. Only a small portion of the meat is eaten fresh; the remainder must be pickled or it will spoil. After the pork is cut into small chunks, it is placed into a pickling jar with salt. When the salt dissolves, sticky rice, wine dregs, pepper, and spices are added. The mixture is then removed from the jar. After being rolled into balls, it is stacked neatly back into the pickling jar.

The Miao also preserve food by smoking. Duck and chicken are considered the choice meats to smoke. Delicacies made with poultry are primarily used for special occasions or for entertaining. On most days, the Miao diet consists of a variety of pickled vegetables such as peppers, beans, eggplant, cucumbers, and radishes, accompanied with a special kind of sour soup.▲

CHAPTER 5

HOLIDAYS AND FESTIVALS

HOLIDAYS CAN REVEAL THE VALUES OF A CULTURE. THE
Miao do not celebrate birthdays or New Year's. Their holidays—
such as the Bridge Holiday, bullfighting competitions, and
Dragon Boat festival—reflect an agricultural society. Miao
holidays are marked by the lunar calendar, a different system
from the 365-day Gregorian calendar. Based on the cycles of
the moon, the lunar calendar has been used by many ancient
cultures to determine agrarian seasons.

The Bridge Holiday

Qing Qiao Jie (ch'ing chow geeyeh), or the Bridge Holiday,
the most celebrated of Miao holidays, takes place on the second
day of the second month of the lunar calendar. On this day,
the Miao repair the many small bridges that link pasture areas.
After the work is finished, the entire community celebrates,
giving offerings of wine and food. The children wear red-dyed
eggs around their necks to mark the occasion. By making a
chore into a social event, the Miao are able to forget the
drudgery of work.

Miao elders are greatly respected within the community.

On holidays the Miao wear festive clothing and silver jewelry in anticipation of the Lusheng Dance.

The high point of a Miao holiday is the Lusheng Dance, or literally "Step of the Lusheng." This event takes place on the sacred Lusheng grounds. People from surrounding villages congregate, dressed in festive garb and silver ornaments, bearing offerings of wine and food.

The Miao wait eagerly for the dancing festivities to begin, displaying an array of embroidered garments and elaborate headdresses. Silver jewelry glistens in the daylight. It is said that Miao women wear 10 to 20 pounds of silver despite their sometimes petite size. A pair of earrings can weigh more than five pounds.

On holidays, Miao women often wear 10 to 20 pounds of silver jewelry.

Before the dance ceremony begins, a few chosen young men shoulder a wooden barrel and circulate from house to house, collecting a bowl of wine from each. When the barrel is filled to the brim, the young men return to the Lusheng grounds, and the ceremonies can officially begin. A group of eight musicians form a Lusheng team. Each member of the team must drink a small bowl of wine before beginning to play. At the first sound of the Lusheng, the participants gather round.

First, a few of the elderly begin to dance. Wearing blue or red silken robes, they dance in a circle around the wine barrel. Later, others follow, stepping to the beat of the music. One after another, more and more people join in. There is stamping and clapping.

The Miao dance to the music of the Lusheng for hours. They form concentric circles around the wine barrel and dance. The innermost circle consists of elderly men, radiating outward to the younger men, elderly women, younger women, teenage girls and boys, and finally small children. In total, there may be as many as 600 or 700 participants.

According to Miao custom, participants in the Lusheng Dance are to dance and drink with gusto. One would never take just a few sips of wine and break from the dance circle. Young adults are expected to offer continuous libations. The Lusheng Dance ceremony begins at noon and does not end until nightfall.

Bullfighting

Bullfighting competitions are festive occasions for the Miao. In the Miao language, bullfighting is called "releasing the bull to battle." The bulls are not pitted against toreadors, but against other bulls. The season for bullfighting is from early summer to autumn. Traditionally, there was a bullfight every 12 days or so, but the number has been reduced.

A bullfight usually takes place in an arena in a low-lying area next to a hill from which spectators can watch. Each village selects ten bulls to compete. Rules and regulations are agreed upon in advance. In general, there are three types of fighting.

In the first type, "capping bulls," two bulls are taken to the center of the arena and placed three yards apart. Each owner pours a bowl of wine over the head of his animal. Then they prod their bulls by slapping their hindquarters. The animals charge toward each other, wildly thrusting their horns. If the fighting is so violent as to draw blood, the bulls are immediately pulled apart, using ropes that have been tied to their hind legs. If one bull is clearly stronger than the other, the bulls are separated long before injury can result.

The second sparring method is called "bulls touching." One bull is wrapped in protective gear. Its head is protected by a straw pad, and on its feet are metal shoes. This bull is placed at the center of the arena. Another bull, placed 20 yards away, is sent charging toward the center. The two animals fight, and when one finally vanquishes the other, the winner is pulled away.

A young Miao woman prepares for the Lusheng Dance.

The Miao Dragon Boat Festival is celebrated during the middle of the fifth month of the lunar calendar.

The third bullfighting method is the most violent and is rarely practiced anymore. Both bulls and their respective owners stand at opposite ends of the arena. The owners set the bulls to charge at each other. In many cases, one of the animals is killed.

After all competitions have taken place, the grand prize bull is crowned with a triangular flag. The owner pours a bowl of wine over the victor's head. The townspeople gather around the bull and its owner, making libations to celebrate the strength of the animal and to praise the owner.

Participants in the Lusheng Dance are expected to celebrate with drink and dance from noon until dusk.

Dragon Boat Festival

The *Longchuan*, or Dragon Boat festival, is an annual event. Dragon Boats are made up of large and small boats joined together. Usually a large vessel, called the motherboat, or *mu-chuan*, is placed between two smaller boats, called childboats, or *zi-chuan*. The bow of the motherboat supports a large dragon head carved from willow wood. The bodies of the vessels are made from fir wood. The Han Chinese race Dragon Boats also and do so in honor of Si Yuan, a famous Chinese poet who supposedly drowned himself. The Miao race Dragon Boats for a different reason. Two legends explain why.

In Guizhou, near the Qing Shui River, there lived a horrible black dragon that had committed every atrocity known to man. The dragon harassed the common folk as they traversed the shores of the river. The people detested the creature and longed to do away with it.

Near the river lived an old fisherman and his son. Father and son were dependent on each other for survival. They fished for a livelihood. One year, during the fifth month, the son was captured by the black dragon while fishing. When the old man discovered that his beloved son was missing, he was furious, knowing that the culprit must surely be the evil dragon. Thereupon, the father gathered firearms and a sword and headed for the dragon's lair.

The lair was dark, deep, and mysterious. The old man finally found the dragon and fought it for nine days and nine nights. Finally he was able to cut the dragon into three pieces, thus rescuing his son. The old man set the lair afire. In the wink of an

At festivals Miao women often display the beautiful garments they have embroidered.

Music plays an important role in Miao celebrations.

eye, the dense smoke that had lined the Qing Shui river lifted, and the shores became peaceful.

One day a Miao woman went to the river bank to fetch water. Carelessly she dropped her ladle into the river and had to get a stick to retrieve it. When the stick hit the dipper, there came a loud clapping sound that caused the sky to light up. Gradually, the darkness lifted and light poured out everywhere.

To commemorate the meritorious deeds of both the fisherman and the young woman, the Miao celebrate Dragon Boat day mid-fifth month of the lunar calendar. While the Dragon Boats are rowed, young men beat drums to recreate the sound of the ladle being retrieved by the stick.▲

CHAPTER 6

A THREATENED CULTURE

THE COLORFUL CULTURE OF THE MIAO OF CHINA HAS
become seriously endangered. Although the Miao retain many
of their traditions, they are gradually being swept up into
mainstream Chinese culture. The policies of the Chinese
government and the Miao's own economic pragmatism are
the two main reasons that minorities in China, including the
Miao, are being assimilated. Miao are migrating in vast
numbers to Special Economic Zones (SEZs) seeking work as
temporary wage laborers.

In an attempt to modernize its economic practices, the
Chinese government has set up these experimental zones
where free enterprise is encouraged. In general, the Chinese
government restricts economic development and has limited,
if any, free enterprise. Young people, regardless of ethnic
background, are flocking to the SEZs. Although they may earn
more money there, they must be apart from their families.
Through this separation from their parents, Miao youth are
learning to become their own decision-makers.

Today, some young Miao choose to live the traditional lifestyle of their villages rather than become a part of the mainstream Chinese culture.

Many of the forests in the mountains of Guizhou have been set aside as Natural Protection Areas to save them from deforestation.

The unfortunate result is that Miao traditions are beginning to be lost. However, the positive aspect of this change is that, as the Miao enter the Chinese mainstream, they and their children will likely have a better chance at improving their economic and political status. Minorities in China, including the Miao, have been brought closer to the rest of Chinese society through education.

Environmental and Social Ills

The Han Chinese and minorities alike have to face global problems of environmental destruction. Many of Guizhou

Environmental protection legislation in China offers some hope for the Miao.

Province's forests have been designated Natural Protection Areas in an effort to conserve resources. Industrialization has brought wealth at the price of deforestation. Future political decisions will undoubtedly affect the Miao.

The Miao have also been shortchanged in the area of social justice. They are a brave people who have made many unappreciated sacrifices in the past. Perhaps the most poignant example of Miao heroism was seen during the late 1960s and '70s, when the United States sought to defeat communism in war-torn Southeast Asia. The United States trained a number of Laotian Hmong as fighter pilots. The Hmong believed they were fighting for their own homes, but they ended up becoming embroiled in the Vietnam War. The Miao lost their homelands to the tragedy of chemical warfare during the war. They are still petitioning Washington today for reparations. ▲

NEIGHBORING PEOPLES

THE SUBJECT OF ETHNIC MINORITIES IN CHINA REMAINS A continuing controversy. The majority ethnic group in China are the **Han**. Throughout history, the Han Chinese have believed in their ability to absorb peoples they considered foreigners. Those who lived outside of the defined political and social boundaries of China were considered barbarians.

If we examine what it entails to be Han Chinese, we find that the distinctions are less physiological than they are social, political, and economic. China was not always ruled by the Han Chinese. The movie *The Last Emperor* depicted the final years of the Ch'ing Dynasty, during which political power was held by the Manchu, a people who came from Northern China. Over the roughly two centuries of the Ch'ing Dynasty (1664-1912), the Manchu adopted many Han ways. Scholars call this gradual process of assimilation "sinicization." In reality, social exchange is rarely a one-way street. The Manchu contributed as much to Han culture as did Han culture to the Manchu.

Miao teenagers use songs to court one another.

Chinese scholars have identified at least 50 ethnic minorities living within the current geographical boundaries of China. It is easy to think of China as one big country, when in fact it has been unified by authoritarian governments.

Many of China's minority groups are challenging the central government to grant them political autonomy, the two foremost being the Tibetans and the Mongolians. Living on the very edge of what is now China's territorial influence, these groups are fighting for independence. Other ethnic minorities of China have not been so outspoken. Having some degree of economic control, these groups live in relative harmony with the Han.

The Miao village of Fan Pa is one of the few villages where the men still wear traditional Miao costume.

On holidays, Miao from many villages celebrate together.

The immediate neighbors of the Miao are the **Dong,** the **Bouyei,** and the **Shui.** The Dong, who number about 1.5 million, make their living primarily from timber resources, which abound in the Hunan-Guizhou-Guanxi border region. The Dong cultivate the fir tree for commercial purposes. Oil is extracted from other trees such as the camellia. The oil is used both for consumption and in varnish. When a child is born, the parents plant fir saplings. These trees are felled when the child marries and are used to build a house for the bride and groom.

Like the Miao, the Dong live in villages populated by several households. Before Communist indoctrination took root in the 1950s, the Dong practiced strict sexual segregation. Girls were sequestered on upper floors of houses and were not allowed to come in contact with men. Women were considered unclean and were forbidden to touch sacrificial objects. Before the birth of her first child, a young bride remained at home, visiting her husband on holidays.

The Bouyei also make their living from timber. They speak a language that belongs to the Sino-Tibetan family of languages. Living in large clans, the Bouyei live in two-story houses. Like the Miao, the Bouyei court each other through song.

The Shui are a very small group. Numbering only about 250,000, they occupy the upper reaches of the Longjiang and Duliu rivers. They live in compact communities. The Shui speak a Chinese dialect in daily life, but they have a special language for religious purposes. They are highly literate, with a written language and an extensive literature of poems and ballads. The Shui have their own calendar, which begins during the ninth month of the traditional lunar calendar. They celebrate their New Year with great pomp and circumstance. ▲

FACTS ABOUT THE MIAO

Population: 7.4 million

Location: Southwestern China, mostly in Guizhou; Cambodia and Laos

Environment: Mountainous regions

Language: Varying languages of the Miao-yao branch of Sino-Tibetan, Cambodian, Laotian

Main Activities: Farming, trading timber with other neighboring minorities, embroidery

Main crops: Rice, maize, potatoes, Chinese sorghum, beans, rape, peanuts, tobacco, ramie, sugar cane, cotton, oil-tea, camellia, and tung tree

Domestic animals: Fowl, pigs

Game Animals: Primarily cultivated fish

GLOSSARY

agrarian Relating to farmers and their way of life.

animist One who believes in spirits.

assimilation Absorption of a people or group into the culture of another people or group.

dearth Scarcity or famine.

dynasty Succession of rulers of the same line of descent.

Han The largest ethnic group in China.

Hmong Splinter group of the Miao. The Hmong migrated from China during the 19th century and now reside in Laos and Cambodia.

libation An act of pouring a liquid or drink as a sacrifice.

Longchuan Dragon Boat.

Lusheng Musical instrument of the Miao, a pipe usually made from a hollowed-out bamboo shoot.

migration Movement from one country or locality to another.

monogamy Practice of having only one spouse at a time.

polytheist Concerning worship of more than one god.

Qing Wiao Jie The Bridge Holiday of the Miao.

shamanism Religion calling for belief in gods, demons, or spirits whom only the shaman can contact.

Special Economic Zone (SEZ) Special region in China where business can be conducted with fewer restrictions than in other areas.

Sin Sai Legendary figure of the Hmong. The Sin Sai legend demonstrates their regional differences from the Miao of China, who do not refer to Sin Sai.

symbiotic Concerning the close and often mutually beneficial association of two dissimilar organisms.

Youfang The Miao courtship ritual.

FOR FURTHER READING

China House Gallery. *Richly Woven Traditions: Costumes of the Miao of Southwest China and Beyond.* New York: China Institute in America, 1987.

China's Minority Nationalities. Beijing: China Reconstructs, 1984.

Lyman, Thomas Amis. *Dictionary of Mong Njua: A Miao Language of Southeast Asia.* The Hague: Mouton, 1974.

Mickey, Margaret Portia. *The Cowrie Shell Miao of Kweichou.* Cambridge: Harvard University Press, 1947.

Monkey (A Chinese Folktale). Arthur Waley, trans. New York: Grove Press, 1943.

Olney, Douglas P. *A Bibliography of the Hmong (Miao) of Southeast Asia and the Hmong Refugees in the United States.* Minneapolis: Southeast Asian Refugee Studies Project, 1983.

INDEX

Photo Credits: ©Anako Editions/Patrick Bernard, Ly Quoc Uy
Design: Kim Sonsky